# The

# Language

# of Love

Other books by

# Blue Mountain Press INC.

# The
# Language
# of Love

Revised Edition
Edited by Susan Polis Schutz
Designed and Illustrated
by Stephen Schutz

**Blue Mountain Press** ™

Boulder, Colorado

Library of Congress Number: 75-13860
ISBN: 0-88396-012-5

Layout by Roger Ben Wilson
Manufactured in the United States of America

First Printing: July, 1975
Second Printing: September, 1975
Third Printing: January, 1976
Fourth Printing: January, 1977
Fifth Printing: March, 1978
Sixth Printing: January, 1979
Seventh Printing: February, 1980

**Blue Mountain Press** INC.

P.O. Box 4549, Boulder, Colorado 80306

## ACKNOWLEDGMENTS

The illustration on page 14 is based on a Chinese print; the Chinese calligraphy on page 17 is by Kyung NamKoong; the illustration on page 22 is based on an ancient Greek vase. All the other illustrations are by Stephen Schutz.

The following poems by Susan Polis Schutz have appeared earlier: "Your heart is my heart" Copyright © Continental Publications, 1971; "The ocean brought me peace" Copyright © Continental Publications, 1971; "When someone cares" Copyright © Continental Publications, 1974.

We gratefully acknowledge the permission granted by the following authors, publishers, and authors' representatives to reprint poems from their publications. Recognition is also made to poets and original publishers for the use of many poems which are now in the public domain.

William Morrow & Co., Inc. for "The Only Song I'm Singing," and "The World Is Not a Pleasant Place to Be," from *MY HOUSE* by Nikki Giovanni. © Copyright 1972 by Nikki Giovanni.

Harcourt, Brace, Jovanovich, Inc. for "i love you much (most beautiful darling)" by E. E. Cummings. © Copyright 1958 by E. E. Cummings. Reprinted from his volume, *COMPLETE POEMS 1913-1962*, by permission of Harcourt, Brace, Jovanovich, Inc.

Harcourt, Brace, Jovanovich, Inc. for "love is the every only god" by E. E. Cummings. © Copyright 1940 by E. E. Cummings; © Copyright 1968 by Marion Morehouse Cummings. Reprinted from *COMPLETE POEMS 1913-1962* by E. E. Cummings by permission of Harcourt, Brace, Jovanovich, Inc.

Norma Millay Ellis for "Ashes of Life" and "The Concert" from *COLLECTED POEMS*, Harper & Row. © Copyright 1917, 1945 by Edna St. Vincent Millay and 1923, 1951 by Edna St. Vincent Millay and Norma Millay Ellis. Reprinted by permission.

A careful effort has been made to trace the ownership of poems used in this anthology in order to get permission to reprint poems and to give proper credit to the copyright owners.

If any error or omission has occurred, it is completely inadvertent, and we would like to correct it in future editions provided that written notification is made to the publisher: BLUE MOUNTAIN PRESS, INC., P.O. Box 4549, Boulder, Colorado 80306.

# CONTENTS

**B**ecause our relationship
is based on
honesty and
fairness,
there is no
need to test
each other.
It is so
wonderful
to find someone
whom I
don't need
to play games
with
and who lives
up to everything that
I consider
important, right and
beautiful

— Susan Polis Schutz

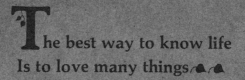

The best way to know life
Is to love many things

## LIGHTED LAMP

Love is something eternal—the aspect may change, but not the essence. There is the same difference in a person before and after he is in love as there is in an unlighted lamp and one that is burning. The lamp was there and it was a good lamp, but now it is shedding light, too, and that is its real function.

Vincent Van Gogh

# LOVE

There is no difficulty that enough love
will not conquer; No disease that enough love
will not heal; No door that enough love
will not open; No gulf that enough love
will not bridge; No wall that enough love
will not throw down; No sin that enough love
will not redeem . . .

It makes no difference how deeply seated
may be the trouble,
How hopeless the outlook,
How muddled the tangle,
How great the mistake,—
A sufficient realization of love will dissolve
it all . . . If only you could love enough,
you would be the happiest and most powerful
being in the world . . .

 Emmet Fox

**L**ove is very patient,
very kind.
Love knows no jealousy;
love makes no parade,
gives itself no airs,
is never rude, never selfish,
never irritated, never resentful
. . . love is gladdened by goodness,
always slow to expose,
always eager to believe the best,
always hopeful, always patient.

Love never disappears.

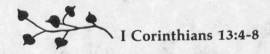

I Corinthians 13:4-8

**H**e who defends with love
will be secure;
Heaven will save him, and
protect him with love

**B**y the accident of fortune a man
  may rule the world for a time,
but by virtue of love he
  may rule the world forever.

**K**indness in words
  creates confidence.
Kindness in thinking
  creates profoundness
Kindness in feeling
  creates love.

Lao Tzu

**O**ur love was pure
        as the snow on the mountains
White as a moon
        between the clouds

Cho Wen-Chun

一部分的土

**T**ake twin mounds of clay
Mold them as you may
Shape one after me,
Another after thee.
Then quickly break them both.
Remix, remake them both—
One formed after thee,
The other after me.

Part of my clay is thine;
Part of thy clay is mine

Kwan Tao-Shing
(13th Century)

**I**s the day better than the night?
Or is the night better than the day?
How can I tell?
But this I know is right:
Both are worth nothing
When my love's away

 Amaru

**A**lthough I have a lamp and fire,
Stars, moon, and sun to give me light,
Unless I look into your eyes,
All is dark night

 Bhartrhari

# सत्री सेह

**A**ll that we are
is the result of what we think.

How then can a man escape being filled with hatred,
if his mind is constantly repeating . . . He misused me,
he hit me, he defeated me, he robbed me—?

Hatred can never put an end to hatred;
hate is conquered only by love

 Buddha

Blow wind, to where my loved one is,
Touch him, and come and touch me soon:
I'll feel his gentle touch through you,
And meet his beauty in the moon.

These things are much for one who loves—
A person can live by them alone—
That he and I breathe the same air,
And that the earth we tread is one

Ramayana

The wind that sweeps down Ikaho
One day it blows, they say,
Another it does not blow
Only my love
Knows no time

 Azumauta

**I**f all the world were mine to plunder
I'd be content with just one town,
And in that town, one house alone,
And in that house, one single room,
And in that room, one cot only,
For there, asleep, is the one I love.

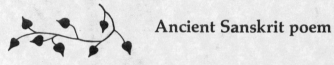

Ancient Sanskrit poem

सर्वी स्नेह

It is a good thing to be
rich and to be strong,
but it is a better thing
to be loved

 Euripides

Of all the creations
of the earth and heaven
love is the most precious

Some say the most beautiful thing
on this dark earth
is a cavalry regiment,
some a battalion of infantry on the march,
and some a fleet of long oars.
But to me the fairest thing is when
one is in love with someone else

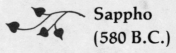 Sappho
(580 B.C.)

23

# אַהֲבָה

**M**any waters cannot quench love,
neither can the floods drown it

　　　Song of Solomon 8:7

**I**ntreat me not to leave thee,
　And to return from following after thee:
For whither thou goest, I will go;
　And where thou lodgest, I will lodge;
Thy people shall be my people,
　And thy God my God;
Where thou diest, will I die,
　And there will I be buried:
The Lord do so to me,
And more also,
　If aught but death part thee and me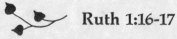

Ruth 1:16-17

**M**y beloved spake, and said unto me,
Rise up, my love, my fair one, and come away.
For, lo, the winter is past,
The rain is over and gone;
The flowers appear on the earth;
The time of the singing of birds is come,
And the voice of the turtle is heard in our land;
The fig tree putteth forth her green figs,
And the vines with the tender grape
Give a good smell.
Arise, my love, my fair one, and come away.

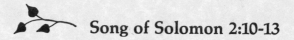 Song of Solomon 2:10-13

. . . a man leaves his father
and mother, and clings to his wife,
and the two become one flesh.

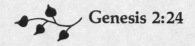 Genesis 2:24

**L**et us not love in word, neither
in tongue; but in deed and in truth.

John 3:18

**L**ove knows no limit to its endurance,
No end to its trust,
No fading of its hope;
It can outlast anything.
Love still stands when
All else has fallen

Corinthians 13:7-8
Phillips Translation

Love consists in this
that two solitudes protect
and touch and greet
each other

**I** am so glad that you are here
it helps me to realize how
beautiful my world is

**T**here is a miracle that happens every time to those
who really love: the more they give, the more
they possess of that precious nourishing love from
which flowers and children have their strength . . .

Rainer Maria Rilke

Doubt that the stars are fire;
Doubt that the sun doth move;
Doubt truth to be a liar;
But never doubt I love

My bounty is as boundless as the sea,
My love as deep; the more I give to thee
The more I have, for both are infinities

# LOVE'S NOT TIME'S FOOL

**L**et me not to the marriage of true minds
Admit impediments. Love is not love
Which alters when it alteration finds,
Or bends with the remover to remove,
O, no! it is an ever-fixed mark,
That looks on tempests and is never shaken;
It is the star to every wandering bark,
Whose worth's unknown, although his height be taken.
Love's not Time's fool, though rosy lips and cheeks
Within his bending sickle's compass come;
Love alters not with his brief hours and weeks,
But bears it out even to the edge of doom.
If this be error and upon me proved,
I never writ, nor no man ever loved

William Shakespeare

# WHEN, IN DISGRACE WITH FORTUNE
# AND MEN'S EYES

When, in disgrace with fortune
   and men's eyes,
I all alone beweep my outcast
   state,
And trouble deaf heaven with my
   bootless cries,
And look upon myself, and curse
   my fate,
Wishing me like to one more
   rich in hope,
Featured like him, like him
   with friends possessed,
Desiring this man's art,
   and that man's scope,
With what I most enjoy contented
   least;
Yet in these thoughts myself
   almost despising,
Haply I think on thee, and
   then my state,
Like to the lark at break
   of day arising
From sullen earth, sings hymns
   at heaven's gate;
For thy sweet love remembered
   such wealth brings
That then I scorn to change my
   state with kings.

# SHALL I COMPARE THEE TO A SUMMER'S DAY?

**S**hall I compare thee to a summer's day?
Thou art more lovely and more temperate:
Rough winds do shake the darling buds of May,
And summer's lease hath all too short a date:
Sometime too hot the eye of heaven shines,
And often is his gold complexion dimm'd;
And every fair from fair sometime declines,
By change or nature's changing course untrimm'd;
But thy eternal summer shall not fade
Nor lose possession of that fair thou owest;
Nor shall Death brag thou wander'st in his shade,
When in eternal lines to time thou growest;
So long as men can breathe or eyes can see,
So long lives this and this gives life to thee.

William Shakespeare

**T**hat love is all
there is
is all we know of love

 Emily Dickinson

# TO MY DEAR AND LOVING HUSBAND

If ever two were one, then surely we.
If ever man were loved by wife, then thee;
If ever wife was happy in a man,
Compare with me, ye women, if you can.
I prize thy love more than whole mines of gold
Or all the riches that the East doth hold.
My love is such that rivers cannot quench,
Nor ought but love from thee, give recompense.
Thy love is such I can no way repay,
The heavens reward thee manifold, I pray.
Then while we live, in love let's so persevere
That when we live no more, we may live ever.

Anne Bradstreet

# THE PASSIONATE SHEPHERD
## TO HIS LOVE

Come live with me and be my Love,
And we will all the pleasures prove
That valleys, groves, hills and fields,
Woods or steepy mountain yields.

And we will sit upon the rocks
Seeing the shepherds feed their flocks.
By shallow rivers, to whose falls
Melodious birds sing madrigals.

And I will make thee beds of roses
And a thousand fragrant posies,
A cap of flowers, and a kirtle
Embroidered all with leaves of myrtle.

A gown made of the finest wool,
Which from our pretty lambs we pull,
Fair lined slippers for the cold,
With buckles of the purest gold.

A belt of straw and ivy buds,
With coral clasps and amber studs:
And if these pleasures may thee move,
Come live with me and be my Love.

The shepherd swains shall dance and sing
For thy delight each May-morning:
If these delights thy mind may move,
Then live with me and be my Love.

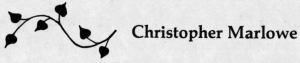

Christopher Marlowe

# WHEN WE TWO PARTED

When we two parted
In silence and tears,
Half broken-hearted,
To sever for years,
Pale grew thy cheek and cold,
Colder thy kiss;
Truly that hour foretold
Sorrow to this!

The dew of the morning
Sunk chill on my brow;
It felt like the warning
Of what I feel now.
Thy vows are all broken,
And light is thy fame:
I hear thy name spoken
And share in its shame.

They name thee before me,
A knell to mine ear;
A shudder comes o'er me—
Why wert thou so dear?
They know not I knew thee
Who knew thee too well:
Long, long shall I rue thee
Too deeply to tell.

In secret we met:
In silence I grieve
That thy heart could forget,
Thy spirit deceive.
If I should meet thee
After long years,
How should I greet thee?—
With silence and tears.

Lord Byron

# MY DELIGHT AND THY DELIGHT

My delight and thy delight
Walking, like two angels white,
In the gardens of the night:

My desire and thy desire
Twining to a tongue of fire,
Leaping live, and laughing higher;

Through the everlasting strife
In the mystery of life.

Love, from whom the world begun,
Hath the secret of the sun.
Love can tell, and love alone,
Whence the million stars were strewn,
Why each atom knows its own,
How, in spite of woe and death,
Gay is life, and sweet is breath:

This he taught us, this we knew,
Happy in his science true,
Hand in hand as we stood
'Neath the shadows of the wood,
Heart to heart as we lay
In the dawning of the day

Robert Bridges

The sea has its pearls
the heaven its stars
But my heart, my heart
my heart has its love

Nature produces
the greatest results
with the simplest
means. These are
simply the sun,
flowers,
water,
and
love

Heinrich Heine

# LOVE IS . . .

. . . the principle of existence and its only end

Benjamin Disraeli

. . . goodness, and honor, and peace and pure living

Henry van Dyke

. . . the enchanted dawn of every heart

Lamartine

. . . the emblem of eternity: it confounds all notion of
time: effaces all memory of a beginning,
all fear of an end

Madame De Stael

# LOVE IS . . .

. . . a trembling happiness

Kahlil Gibran

. . . like a lovely rose, the world's delight

Christina Rossetti

. . . the dawn of civility and grace

Ralph Waldo Emerson

. . . the exchange of two fantasies and the contact of
two skins

Nicholas Chamfort

# LOVE IS . . .

. . . to the moral nature exactly what the sun is to
   the earth

Balzac

. . . the master key that opens the gates of happiness

Oliver Wendell Holmes

. . . a second life; it grows into the soul,
warms every vein, and beats in every pulse

Joseph Addison

. . . the beauty of the soul

St. Augustine

# LOVE IS ...

. . . light from heaven; A spark of that immortal fire

Lord Byron

. . . the Mother of Art, inspirer of poet, patriot, and philosopher

. . . the magician, the enchanter, that changes worthless things to joy

Robert Ingersoll

# YOU AND I

**M**y hand is lonely for your clasping, dear;
　My ear is tired waiting for your call.
I want your strength to help, your laugh to cheer;
　Heart, soul and senses need you, one and all.
I droop without your full, frank sympathy;
　We ought to be together—you and I;
We want each other so, to comprehend
　The dream, the hope, things planned, or seen,
　　or wrought.
Companion, comforter and guide and friend,
　As much as love asks love, does thought ask thought.
Life is so short, so fast the lone hours fly,
　We ought to be together, you and I

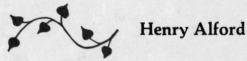

Henry Alford

# THE ONLY SONG I'M SINGING

they tell me that i'm beautiful i know
i'm Black and proud
the people ask for autographs
i sometimes draw a crowd
i've written lots of poetry and other
kinds of books
i've heard that white men crumble
from one of my mean looks
i study hard and know my facts
in fact the truth is true
the only song i'm singing now is my song
of you
   and i'm asking you baby please
   please somehow show me what i need
   to know so i can love you right
   now
i've had great opportunities to move
the world around
whenever they need love and truth they call
me to their town
the president he called me up and asked
me to come down

but if you think you want me home i think
i'll stick around
   and i'm asking you baby
   please baby baby show me
   right now most of the things i need to know
   so i can love you somehow

Nikki Giovanni
(8 jan 72)

## THE WORLD IS NOT
## A PLEASANT PLACE TO BE

the world is not a pleasant place
to be without
someone to hold and be held by

a river would stop
its flow if only
a stream were there
to receive it

an ocean would never laugh
if clouds weren't there
to kiss her tears

the world is not
a pleasant place to be without
someone

Nikki Giovanni
(17 feb 72)

i love you much(most beautiful darling)

more than anyone on the earth and i
like you better than everything in the sky

—sunlight and singing welcome your coming

although winter may be everywhere
with such a silence and such a darkness
noone can quite begin to guess

(except my life)the true time of year—

and if what calls itself a world should have
the luck to hear such singing(or glimpse such
sunlight as will leap higher than high
through gayer than gayest someone's heart at your each

nearerness)everyone certainly would(my
most beautiful darling)believe in nothing but love

love is the every only god

who spoke this earth so glad and big
even a thing all small and sad
man,may his mighty briefness dig

for love beginning means return
seas who could sing so deep and strong

one queerying wave will whitely yearn
from each last shore and home come young

so truly perfectly the skies
by merciful love whispered were,
completes its brightness with your eyes

any illimitable star

e. e. cummings

Love does not consist
in gazing at each other,
but in looking outward
in the same direction.

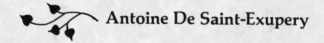 Antoine De Saint-Exupery

# MEETING AT NIGHT

The gray sea and the long black land;
And the yellow half-moon large and low;
And the startled little waves that leap
In fiery ringlets from their sleep,
As I gain the cove with pushing prow,
And quench its speed in the slushy sand.

Then a mile of warm sea-scented beach;
Three fields to cross till a farm appears;
A tap at the pane, the quick sharp scratch
And blue spirt of a lighted match,
And a voice less loud, through its joys and fears,
Than the two hearts beating each to each!

**O**utside are the storms and strangers: we—
Oh, close, safe, warm sleep I and she,
—I and she!

**C**hance cannot change my love,
    nor time impair.

**W**hat's the earth
With all its art, verse, music, worth
Compared with love, found, gained and kept?

Robert Browning

How do I love thee? Let me count the ways.
I love thee to the depth and breadth and height
My soul can reach, when feeling out of sight
For the ends of Being and ideal Grace.
I love thee to the level of everyday's
Most quiet need, by sun and candle-light.
I love thee freely, as men strive for Right;
I love thee purely, as they turn from Praise.
I love thee with the passion put to use
In my old griefs, and with my childhood's faith.
I love thee with a love I seemed to lose
With my lost saints,—I love thee with the breath,
Smiles, tears, of all my life!—and, if God choose,
I shall but love thee better after death.

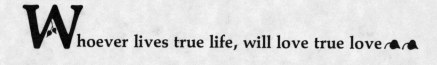

Whoever lives true life, will love true love.

Elizabeth Barrett Browning

**W**hat the heart has once owned and had, it shall never lose.

**O**f all earthly music, that which reaches the farthest into heaven is the beating of a loving heart.

Love is the river of life in this world.
Think not that ye know it who stand at the
little tinkling rill, the first small fountain.

Not until you have gone through the rocky
gorges, and not lost the stream; not until you
have gone through the meadow, and the stream
has widened and deepened until fleets could ride
on its bosom; not until beyond the meadow
you have come to the unfathomable ocean,
and poured your treasures into its depths—
not until then can you know what love is.

Henry Ward Beecher

Spring bursts today
For Love is risen
And all the earth's at play

# A BIRTHDAY

My heart is like a singing bird
Whose nest is in a water'd shoot;
My heart is like an appletree
Whose boughs are bent with thick-set fruit;
My heart is like a rainbow shell
That paddles in a halcyon sea;
My heart is gladder than all these,
Because my love is come to me.
Raise me a dais of silk and down:
Hang it with fair and purple dyes;
Carve it in doves and pomegranates,
And peacocks with a hundred eyes;
Work it in gold and silver grapes,
In leaves and silver fleurs-de-lys;
Because the birthday of my life
Is come, my love is come to me.

Christina Rossetti

I am drunk with the happiness
love can give
I never knew how exciting it
could be to live

T he world affairs are many
the important matters are few
the flow of light in the darkness
the feeling of warmth in the cold
and above all the knowledge of love
to fill the great void

 David Polis

Once I knew the depth where no hope was and darkness lay on the face of all things. Then love came and set my soul free. Once I fretted and beat myself against the wall that shut me in. My life was without a past or future, and death a consummation devoutly to be wished. But a little word from the fingers of another fell into my hands that clutched at emptiness, and my heart leaped up with the rapture of living. I do not know the meaning of the darkness, but I have learned the overcoming of it

Helen Keller

# ASHES OF LIFE

Love has gone and left me and the days are all alike;
Eat I must, and sleep I will,—and would that night
 were here!
But ah!—to lie awake and hear the slow hours strike!
Would that it were day again!—with twilight near!

Love has gone and left me and I don't know what to do;
This or that or what you will is all the same to me;
But all the things that I begin I leave before I'm through,—
There's little use in anything as far as I can see.

Love has gone and left me,—and the neighbours knock
 and borrow,
And life goes on forever like the gnawing of a mouse,—
And tomorrow and tomorrow and tomorrow and
 tomorrow
There's this little street and this little house.

                              Edna St. Vincent Millay

# THE CONCERT

No, I will go alone.
I will come back when it's over.
Yes, of course I love you.
No, it will not be long.
Why may you not come with me? —
You are too much my lover.
You would put yourself
Between me and song.

If I go alone,
Quiet and suavely clothed,
My body will die in its chair,
And over my head a flame,
A mind that is twice my own,
Will mark with icy mirth
The wise advance and retreat
Of armies without a country,
Storming a nameless gate,
Hurling terrible javelins down
From the shouting walls of a singing town

Where no women wait!
Armies clean of love and hate,
Marching lines of pitiless sound
Climbing hills to the sun and hurling
Golden spears to the ground!
Up the lines a silver runner
Bearing a banner whereon is scored
The milk and steel of a bloodless wound
Healed at length by the sword!

You and I have nothing to do with music.
We may not make of music a filigree frame,
Within which you and I,
Tenderly glad we came,
Sit smiling, hand in hand.

Come now, be content.
I will come back to you, I swear I will;
And you will know me still.
I shall be only a little taller
Than when I went.

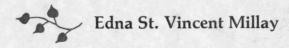

Edna St. Vincent Millay

Every soul is a celestial Venus
to every other soul . . . Love is our highest
word, and the synonym of God

## EROS

The sense of the world is short,—
Long and various the report,—
  To love and be beloved;
Men and gods have not outlearned it;
And, how oft soe'er they've turned it,
  'Tis not to be improved

Ralph Waldo Emerson

# I LOVE YOU

I love your lips when they're wet with wine
  And red with a wild desire;
I love your eyes when the lovelight lies
  Lit with a passionate fire.
I love your arms when the warm white flesh
  Touches mine in a fond embrace;
I love your hair when the strands enmesh
  Your kisses against my face.

Not for me the cold, calm kiss
  Of a virgin's bloodless love;
Not for me the saint's white bliss,
  Nor the heart of a spotless dove.
But give me the love that so freely gives
  And laughs at the whole world's blame,
With your body so young and warm in my arms
  It sets my poor heart aflame.
So kiss me sweet with your warm wet mouth,
  Still fragrant with ruby wine,
And say with a fervor born of the South
  That your body and soul are mine.
Clasp me close in your warm young arms,
  While the pale stars shine above,
And we'll live our whole young lives away
  In the joys of a living love

Ella Wheeler Wilcox

**I** love you
not as something private
and personal, which is my own,
but as something universal
and worthy of love
which I have found

Henry David Thoreau

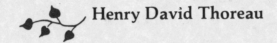

**I** love you
the more in that I believe
you have liked me for my
own sake and for nothing else

John Keats

# I LOVE YOU

**I** love you,
Not only for what you are
But for what I am
When I am with you.

I love you
Not only for what
You have made of yourself
But for what
You are making of me.

I love you
for the part of me
That you bring out;
I love you
For putting your hand
Into my heaped-up heart
And passing over
All the foolish, weak things
That you can't help
Dimly seeing there,
And for drawing out
Into the light
All the beautiful belongings
That no one else had looked
Quite far enough to find.

I love you because you

Are helping me to make
Of the lumber of my life
Not a tavern
But a temple;
Out of works
Of my every day
Not a reproach
But a song.

I love you
Because you have done
More than any creed
Could have done
To make me good,
And more than any fate
Could have done
To make me happy.

You have done it
Without a touch,
Without a word,
Without a sign.

You have done it
By being yourself.
Perhaps that is what
Being a friend means,
After all.

Roy Croft

**L**ove has power to give in
a moment what toil can scarcely
reach in an age

**L**ove does not dominate;
it cultivates

**I**t is the true season
of Love
When we know that
we alone can love,
that no one could ever
have loved before us
and that no one
will ever Love
in the same way
after us

Johann Wolfgang Von Goethe

**S**ome people are always alone
I was, until I met you

Some people can not trust others
I could not, until I met you

Some people are not able to appreciate the flowers
   and trees
I could not, until I met you

Some people are always dissatisfied
I was, until I met you

Some people can not find peace
I could not, until I met you

Some people are never able to experience a sincere love
I could not,
until
I
met
you

**W**hen someone cares
it is easier to speak
it is easier to listen
it is easier to play
it is easier to work
when someone cares
it is easier to laugh

Susan Polis Schutz

The ocean brought me peace
the wind gave me energy
the sun warmed my spirit
the flowers showed me life
but you made me feel

love

Y our heart is my heart
your truth is my truth
your feeling is my feeling

But the real strength of our love
is that we share rather than
control each other's lives

Susan Polis Schutz